Tweet It!

Twitter Projects for the Real World

Carolyn Bernhardt

abdopublishing.com

Published by Abdo Publishing, a division of ABDO, PO Box 398166, Minneapolis, Minnesota 55439. Copyright © 2017 by Abdo Consulting Group, Inc. International copyrights reserved in all countries. No part of this book may be reproduced in any form without written permission from the publisher. Checkerboard Library™ is a trademark and logo of Abdo Publishing.

Printed in the United States of America, North Mankato, Minnesota

062016
092016

Content Developer: Nancy Tuminelly
Design and Production: Mighty Media, Inc.
Series Editor: Liz Salzmann
Photo Credits: iStockphoto; Mighty Media, Inc.; National Park Foundation; National Park Service; Shutterstock; US Department of the Interior

The following manufacturers/names appearing in this book are trademarks: Elmer's®, Office Depot®, Sharpie®, Stanley® Bostitch®, Westcott™

Publishers Cataloging-in-Publication Data
Names: Bernhardt, Carolyn, author.
Title: Tweet it! : Twitter projects for the real world / by Carolyn Bernhardt.
Description: Minneapolis, MN : Abdo Publishing, [2017] | Series: Cool social media | Includes bibliographical references and index.
Identifiers: LCCN 2016936502 | ISBN 9781680783612 (lib. bdg.) | ISBN 9781680790290 (ebook)
Subjects: LCSH: Twitter (Firm)--Juvenile literature. | Twitter--Juvenile literature. | Online social networks--United States--Juvenile literature. | Internet industry--United States--Juvenile literature. | Internet security measures--Juvenile literature.
Classification: DDC 338.4--dc23
LC record available at /http://lccn.loc.gov/2016936502

Contents

What Is Twitter?

You're at a family dinner when your dad tells a funny joke. Everyone is laughing and having a blast! Your brother decides to share the joke with his friends. He logs in to Twitter and writes a tweet about the joke. Instantly, your brother's Twitter followers are in on the joke. Many retweet it to their followers. Soon, your dad's silly joke is being spread around the Internet. This is the power of Twitter!

Twitter is a content-sharing website and app. Users post **status updates** of 140 characters or less. These posts are called tweets and are meant to be short. Some social media users find longer posts on other sites to be overwhelming. Twitter users share brief bits of information quickly. They can also include photos, videos, and article links in their tweets.

The Twitter community connects by following one another. If a Twitter user follows another user, he or she will see that person's posts in his or her feed. Users **tag** each other in tweets and comment on posts. They also retweet, or share, one another's content. This is how tweets can go **viral**. Some tweets are shared around the world by billions of people in just minutes!

Twitter
Site Bytes

Purpose: sharing information, photos, and videos

Type of Service: website and app
URL: www.twitter.com
App name: Twitter

Date of Founding: March 2006

Founders: Jack Dorsey, Evan Williams, and Christopher "Biz" Stone

Compatible Devices:

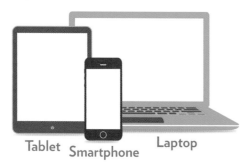

Tablet Smartphone Laptop

Tech Terms:

Tweet

A tweet is the name of a Twitter post. It can contain up to 140 text characters, several images, and video.

Retweet

A retweet is a tweet created by a Twitter user that is reposted by another user.

Hashtag

Hashtags can be included in tweets. A hashtag is a hash symbol (#) followed by a word or phrase. The hashtag becomes a link that groups tweets together. Clicking on the hashtag takes a user to all posts with that hashtag.

Founding **Twitter**

Twitter was founded by Jack Dorsey, Evan Williams, and Christopher "Biz" Stone. The three men were working at a company named Odeo. Dorsey first thought of the idea for Twitter. He wanted to create a way to share short **status updates**.

Dorsey told this idea to Williams and Stone. The trio created the first **version** of Twitter in 2006. At first, only other Odeo employees could use Twitter, and they loved it! The founders soon decided to make Twitter **available** to the public. Today, there are more than 320 million active Twitter users.

Evan Williams

Christopher "Biz" Stone

Jack Dorsey

Account Info:

- ❤ Users must be at least 13 to create an account.

- ❤ Once a user creates an account, he or she chooses a username. This is known as his or her handle. It consists of the @ symbol followed by the username.

- ❤ Users fill out the bio section of their Twitter pages with brief pieces of information about themselves.

- ❤ Users find friends by searching for their usernames, and then follow them. Private users must approve followers before the followers can see their tweets and profile. Public users let their tweets be seen by everyone.

- ❤ Tweets can be up to 140 characters long. This includes spaces.

- ❤ Users can tweet up to two photos at a time or a video up to six seconds long.

Supplies

Here are some of the materials, tools, and devices you'll need for projects in this book.

craft foam

index cards

craft glue

scissors

notebook

timer

pin backs

stapler

hole punch

magnetic tape

permanent markers

printer (loaded with paper and ink)

Staying Safe

The Internet is a great resource for information. And using it can be a lot of fun! But staying safe **online** is most important. Follow these tips to use social media safely.

* Never try to sign up for a social media account if you are underage. Twitter users must be at least 13 years old.

* Don't share personal information online, especially information people can use to find you in real life. This includes your telephone number and home address.

* Be kind online! Remember that real people post content on the Internet. Do not post rude, hurtful, or mean comments. Report any instances of **cyberbullying** you see to a trusted adult.

* In addition to cyberbullying, report any **inappropriate** content to a trusted adult.

Safety Symbols

Some projects in this book require searching on the Internet. Others require the use of hot tools. That means these projects need some adult help. Determine if you'll need help on a project by looking for these safety symbols.

Hot!
This project requires use of a hot tool.

Internet Use
This project requires searching on the Internet.

9

Twitter Charades

Make a game using Twitter
message limitations!

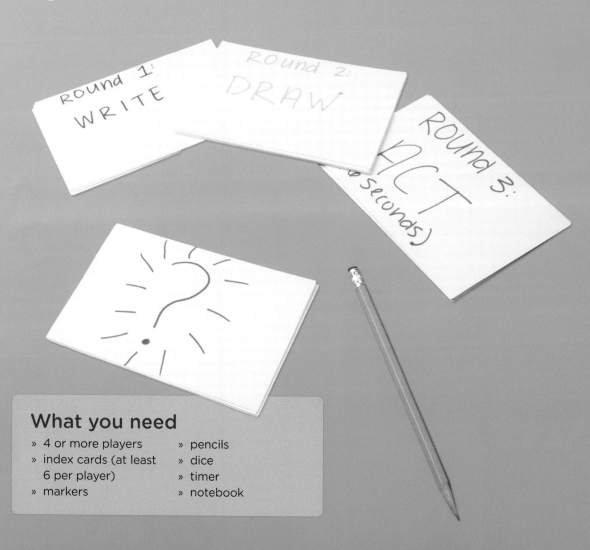

What you need

- » 4 or more players
- » index cards (at least 6 per player)
- » markers
- » pencils
- » dice
- » timer
- » notebook

Twitter's 140-character limit causes users to think creatively about their posts. They need to express an idea or thought in a clear way within the allowed space. Many users post photo and six-second video tweets as well. Could you explain an idea or phrase within these limitations? What if you also could not use certain key words? Create a game of **charades** and find out! Get friends and family members to guess what's on your mind using one drawing, six seconds of acting, or 140 characters or less.

1. Write a question mark (?) on one side of half of the index cards.

2. Divide the remaining index cards into three equal **stacks**. Write "Round 1: Write" on one side of the cards in one stack. On the other side, draw 140 short lines. They will help the players count characters during the game.

3. Write "Round 2: Draw" on one side of the cards in the second stack.

4. Write "Round 3: Act (6 seconds)" on one side of the cards in the third stack.

(continued on the next page)

5. Divide the players into two teams. Give each player a pencil and three ? cards. Have each player write a person, place, or thing on the blank side of each card. Make sure the players keep their words hidden.

6. Place the Round 1, Round 2, and Round 3 cards in separate **stacks**. Set the ? cards next to them.

7. Have each player roll the dice. Whoever rolls the highest number goes first. Set the timer for 2 minutes.

8. For Round 1, the first player draws a ? card and a Round 1 card. He or she reads the word on the ? card but doesn't let the others know what it is.

9. Start the timer. The player has 2 minutes to write a **description** of the word on the Round 1 card. The player may not use the actual word in the description. The player has to do it in 140 characters or less. Don't forget that spaces count as characters.

10. When the time is up, the player shows everyone the description. The first player to guess the word gets a point for his or her team. Write the score in a notebook.

11. Repeat steps 8 through 10 until each player has completed Round 1.

12. For Round 2, the first player draws a ? card and a Round 2 card. He or she has 2 minutes to create a drawing that represents the secret word. When the timer is up, the player shows everyone the drawing. The first player to guess the word wins a point for his or her team. Repeat until everyone has taken a turn.

13. For Round 3, the first player draws a ? card and a Round 3 card. He or she has 2 minutes to think of a way to act out the word in 6 seconds. The player can take notes on the Round 3 card.

14. Then the player acts out the word for the group. Use the timer to keep the performance to 6 seconds. The first player to guess the word wins a point for his or her team. Continue until everyone has taken a turn.

15. Play the game until you run out of cards. Or, create more cards and keep playing!

12

14

Home Hashtags

Come up with creative hashtags for your favorite things and activities at home!

What you need

- » notebook
- » pencil
- » craft foam
- » permanent markers
- » scissors
- » magnetic tape
- » pin backs
- » hot glue gun & glue sticks
- » clear tape

Hashtags are used on many social media sites today. But they began on Twitter! A hashtag is a great way to briefly state a feeling or idea. Create hashtag labels to express your feelings about things, areas, and activities around your house!

1. Think about what you love about your home. Maybe it's a favorite book, framed photo, or couch. Or, think of the rooms in your house you use the most and what you use them for. This could include the kitchen, used for tasty snacking. Or the living room, used for family game or movie nights! List your ideas in a notebook.

2. Think of a creative hashtag for each idea. For example, a framed photo of you in your backyard could be labeled #greatoutdoors. Your living room couch could have a #movienight hashtag. And your refrigerator could have a #yum hashtag. Write your ideas in the notebook.

(continued on the next page)

1

2

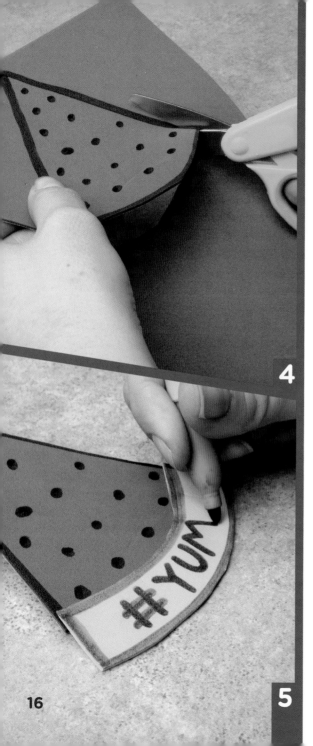

3. Think about fun shapes or drawings that could go with the hashtags. For the backyard photo hashtag #greatoutdoors, this could be a tree. The #yum refrigerator hashtag could be a watermelon slice. Write your ideas in the notebook.

4. Choose one of the ideas from your list. Draw the shape on craft foam. Cut it out and decorate it.

5. Write the hashtag on the shape.

6. When your hashtag label is complete, determine where it will go. Is it meant for the refrigerator? Attach magnetic tape to the back. If your hashtag is for a stuffed animal, backpack, or other cloth item, glue on a pin back. Use clear tape to attach hashtags to other items. Be sure to get **permission** first!

7. Place your hashtags on the items they go with. Change them whenever you like, or as new ideas strike!

#funfact

The Twitter logo is a blue bird. The bird's official name is Larry Bird. He is named after the famous Boston Celtics basketball player of the same name.

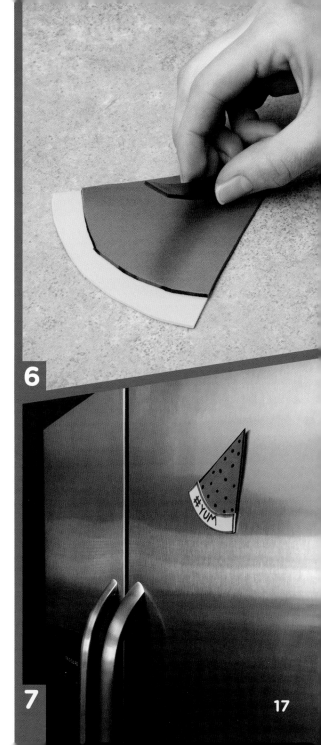

6

7

17

Retweet
Masterpiece

Create something new with old tweets!

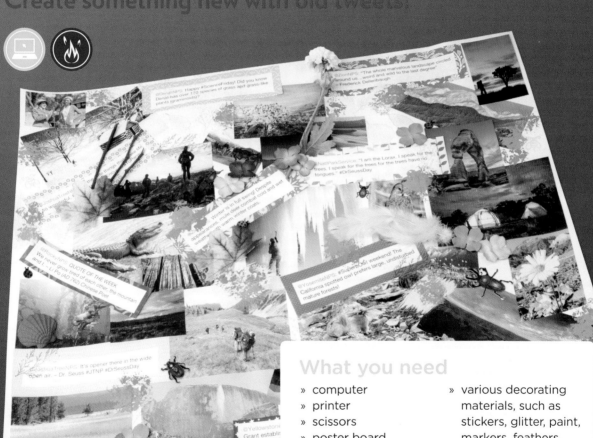

What you need

- » computer
- » printer
- » scissors
- » poster board
- » craft glue
- » hot glue gun & glue sticks
- » various decorating materials, such as stickers, glitter, paint, markers, feathers, leaves & flowers

Twitter is an ongoing conversation between millions of users about endless topics! Users are exposed to new ideas, learn new facts, and see cool images and videos on the site. Combine cool facts, phrases, and images from popular Twitter users to create an amazing poster!

1. Choose a topic from the list below. Then, with adult help, visit the Twitter accounts listed for your topic. Or, have an adult help you research other fun and kid-friendly topics on Twitter.

Animals:

National Geographic Kids: @NGKids
Monterey Bay Aquarium: @MontereyAq
Mission Blue: @MissionBlue

Cartoons:

PBS Kids: @PBSKIDS
Plum Landing: @PlumLandingPBS

Space:

NASA: @NASA
Scott Kelly: @StationCDRKelly
Tim Peake: @astro_timpeake

Travel:

National Park Service: @NatlParkService
National Geographic Travel: @NatGeoTravel

(continued on the next page)

2. Look for cool facts, funny tweets, and amazing images on the Twitter accounts. Print out the ones you like best.

3. Cut out the words and images you printed.

4. Arrange the pieces on the poster board. When you are happy with the design, glue them down.

5. Decorate your poster! Add stickers, glue on feathers, paint designs, and more. Draw images or add glitter. Make your poster really exciting!

6. When your poster is dry, hang it up for everyone to see! See what people can learn from the bits of information in your work of art!

Every Letter Counts

Scramble up letter tiles to quickly create cool tweets!

What you need

- » 2 or more players
- » letter tiles
- » paper
- » scissors
- » markers
- » large container
- » timer
- » notebook
- » pencil

Because tweets have a 140-character limit, Twitter users have to choose their words carefully. Use letter tiles and a timer to test how fast you can create tweets!

1. Gather letter tiles from old board games.

2. Give each player the same number of tiles.

3. Cut some paper into strips.

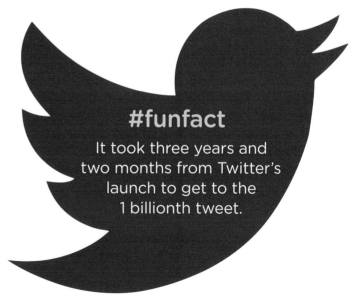

#funfact

It took three years and two months from Twitter's launch to get to the 1 billionth tweet.

4. Divide the strips among the players. Then, have the players write one topic on each of their strips. Put everyone's strips in the container.

5. Set the timer to 2 minutes.

6. Have one player draw a piece of paper out of the container. He or she should announce the topic to the other players.

7. Start the timer. Each player quickly uses his or her tiles to write a tweet about the topic. It could be a phrase or hashtag.

8. When the time is up, have the players show their tweets to the group. Each player then adds up the number of tiles he or she used. That is the player's score for the round. Record the scores in a notebook. The first player to 140 points wins!

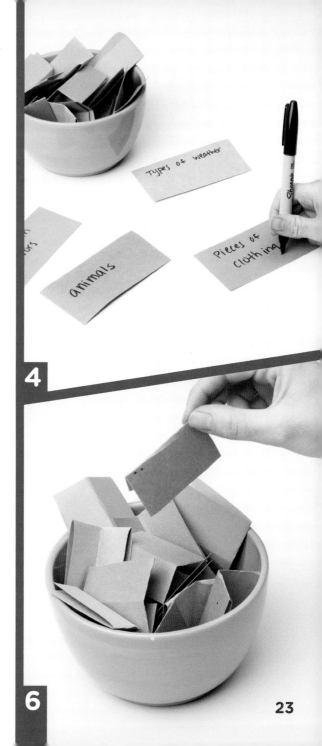

#rewrite

Rewrite your favorite book, play, or film,
140 characters at a time!

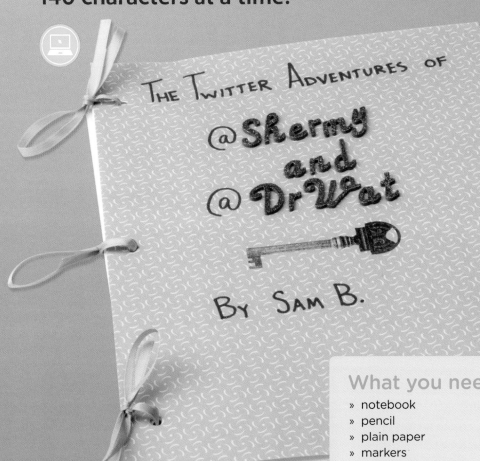

What you need

- » notebook
- » pencil
- » plain paper
- » markers
- » optional: computer, printer, craft glue
- » hole punch
- » card stock
- » ribbon or string
- » scissors
- » various decorating materials, such as stickers, glitter, paint pens & markers

1. Choose a favorite book, play, or film that you know well. Write down all the characters from the story. Give each a Twitter handle, such as @peterpan. This will be how the character is referred to throughout your rewrite. You may want to create a Twitter handle called **@narrator** to tweet sections without **dialogue**. If needed, reread or rewatch your chosen work for reminders or ideas.

2. Next, think about the story. Write down the main plot, actions, and events in your notebook.

3. Divide the story into chapters based on main story points. In your notebook, write down the main characters that appear in each chapter. Then, write down the key things these characters say or do in that chapter. Create lists for each part of the story.

4. Once your lists are complete, you are ready to #rewrite! Write your story on plain paper. Review your notes on each chapter. For each item on the list, create a tweet from one of the characters in the story. Write the story similar to a **script**.

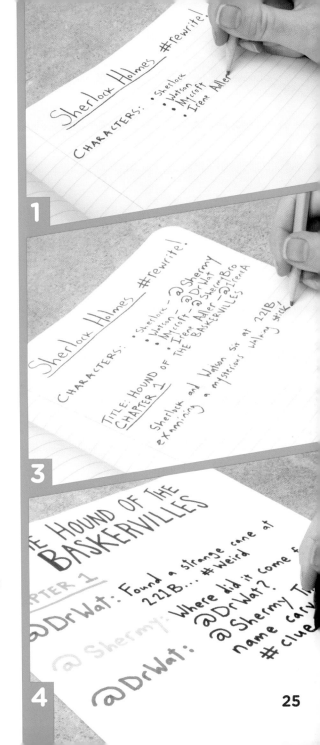

(continued on the next page)

6

7

5. Remember that each tweet must have 140 characters or less. Try including hashtags. They can help cut down on character count. Use as many pages as needed to retell the story.

6. You can include drawings or photos to go along with your tweets. Have an adult help you search for images **online** and print them out. Or, draw images right on the pages.

7. When your rewrite is complete, put the pages in order. Draw three marks along the left edge of the top page. Punch a hole through all of the pages at each mark.

8. Place the pages on top of two pieces of card stock. Make a mark on the card stock through each hole. Then set the pages aside and punch a hole through both sheets of card stock at each mark. Place the pages between the sheets of card stock. Make sure the holes line up.

9. Cut three short pieces of ribbon or string. Tie each one through one punched hole. Tie them loosely so the pages can turn.

10. Design your book's cover. Think of a fun title and write it on the cover. List yourself as the author. Then add designs or other decorations.

11. Show your book to your friends and family members. Were they able to follow the story? What did they think of your rewrite? Think of other stories you could tell in tweets and create more #rewrite books!

9

10

Chain of Tweets

Turn a favorite event or memory
into a cool chain of tweets!

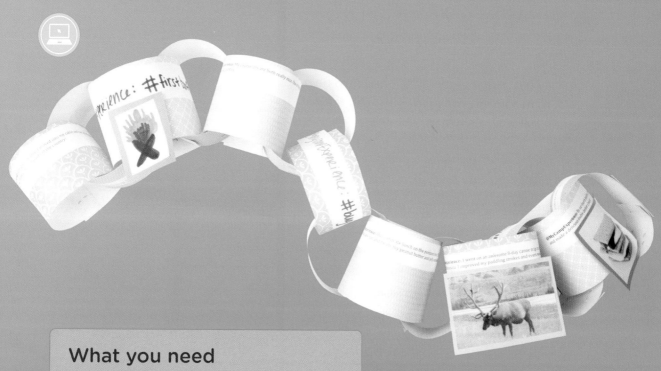

What you need

- » notebook
- » pencil
- » computer
- » word-processing
  program
- » printer
- » markers
- » scissors
- » colored paper
- » craft glue
- » stapler

Twitter is known for communicating breaking news and events as they unfold. News outlets, organizations, and individuals tweet information as things happen. This allows users to follow an event step by step. Think of an exciting or interesting event from your life. Then break it into steps. Create a chain of tweets that tells the story in order, just as it occurred!

1. Pick a past event or memory. This could be a summer at camp or a time you volunteered at a local soup kitchen.

2. In a notebook, write down the important moments from your experience. List them in **chronological** order.

3. Type a tweet for each moment in a word-processing program on your computer. Print out the tweets. You could also handwrite some tweets with markers.

4. Cut the tweets into strips. Glue the tweets to colored paper. Cut each strip out, so the colored paper creates a border.

(continued on the next page)

5. Print out photos to include with some of your tweets. They can be your own photos or ones you find **online** with adult help. Or, you can draw pictures for the tweets.

6. Glue the photos to the tweets they go with. Let the glue dry.

7. Curl the first tweet into a loop with the photo facing out. Staple the ends together.

8. Stick the second tweet through the first loop. Curl it into a loop with the photo facing out. Staple the ends together. Continue adding tweets this way to make a **chronological** chain.

9. Hang your chain in your room or around the house. Revisit the memory any time by reading the chain of tweets!

Glossary

available – able to be had or used.

charades – a game in which one person acts something out and the others have to guess what it is.

chronological – arranged in or according to the order of time.

cyberbully – to tease, hurt, or threaten someone online.

description – a statement that explains how something looks, behaves, or works.

dialogue – a written conversation between two or more characters.

inappropriate – not suitable, fitting, or proper.

narrator – the voice in a story that provides information.

online – connected to the Internet.

permission – when a person in charge says it's okay to do something.

script – the written text for a performance.

stack – a pile of things placed one on top of the other.

status update – a post on social media that describes what the poster is doing or feeling.

tag – to add a name or location to an online post.

version – a different form or type of an original.

viral – quickly or widely spread, usually by electronic communication.

Websites

To learn more about Cool Social Media, visit **booklinks.abdopublishing.com**. These links are routinely monitored and updated to provide the most current information available.

Index